VIDEOGAMES

Rhianna Pratchett

CLASH
by ticktock

Copyright © ticktock Entertainment Ltd 2008

First published in Great Britain in 2008 by ticktock Media Ltd,
2 Orchard Business Centre, North Farm Road, Tunbridge Wells, Kent, TN2 3XF

project editor and picture researcher: Ruth Owen
ticktock project designer: Sara Greasley

With thanks to series editors Honor Head and Jean Coppendale.

Thank you to Lorraine Petersen and the members of nasen

ISBN 978 1 84696 749 8 pbk

Printed in China

Picture credits (t=top; b=bottom; c=centre; l=left; r=right):Courtesy Auravision, Inc.: 16, 17. Courtesy Ralph H. Baer: 6-7
(all). © 2004-2008 Blizzard Entertainment, Inc.: OFCcl, 12, 13, 14-15. British Board of Film Classification: 21c (x2).
DigiPen Institute of Technology: 24. © 2005-2008 Double Fine Productions: 2-3, 22, 23. Courtesy of EA SPORTS:
OFCcr. Heavenly Sword™ ©2007 Sony Computer Entertainment Europe. Heavenly Sword is a trademark of Sony
Computer Entertainment Europe. All rights reserved: 19b. id Software: OFCtl, 11b. Introversion Software: 28-29 (main),
28tl, 28tr. Lara Croft Tomb Raider imagery used under license of Eidos Interactive Limited: OFCtr, 18. Microsoft: OFCc,
OFCb, 4-5, 8, 9t; 9b. © Picture Contact/Alamy: 26-27. Rex Features: 19t. Shutterstock: OFCtc, 1, 8-9c, 21t, 21b, 31t.
Splash Damage: 10, 11t. Ticktock Media Archive: 5t. © Valve Corporation. Used with Permission: 25.

Contents

CHAPTER 1

THE BIRTH OF VIDEOGAMES

If you're reading this, then you must like videogames! But did you know that the first game was created back in 1962? It was called *Spacewar!*

Halo 3 is the third title in Bungie's famous FPS (First-Person Shooter) series.

The objective of *Spacewar!* was to shoot down your opponent's spaceship.

Now fast-forward to 2007 and the release of *Halo 3*. It sold £86 million worth of copies in 24 hours!

Spacewar!

Spacewar! to Halo 3 in 45 years. Just think what might happen in the next 45!

CHAPTER 2 **CONSOLE GAMING**

In 1972, the world got its first console, the Magnavox Odyssey.

This funny-looking collection of boxes was designed by Ralph H. Baer. He is known as the "Father of Videogames".

"Brown Box"

The "Brown Box" was the prototype for the Magnavox Odyssey. Imagine trying to fit that under your TV!

The Magnavox Odyssey may have sounded like one of the Transformers, but it finally brought videogames into people's homes. Without it, we may not have had an Xbox 360, a PS3 or a Wii.

A 1972 ad for the Magnavox Odyssey

Console

Hand controller

Plug-in game programming carts

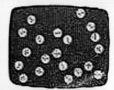

Shooting Gallery screenshots

Baer also created the first peripheral. It was a light-gun for an Odyssey game called *Shooting Gallery*.

CHAPTER 3 ONLINE GAMING

SEGA's Dreamcast was the first console with a built-in modem. This meant it could properly support online gaming.

Dreamcast made multiplayer games, such as *Phantasy Star Online*, extremely popular.

When Sony released a network adapter for the PS2, it allowed players all over the world to voice chat through a headset.

Headset

But it wasn't until the release of Xbox Live for Xbox and the Xbox 360, that online console gaming really took off in a big way.

Xbox Live now has over 8 million players worldwide.

Online gaming has always had a big following on the PC.

It began with games such as *Quake 3* and *Unreal Tournament*.

A Quake clan gets together to play.

These games produce large groups of fans. The fans create forums and clans.

They often use online tools and editors to create their own mods (modifications), maps and missions for the games they love.

Making a map or level is a great way to learn how games are created.

Splash Damage at work

Splash Damage is a company that develops games.

They started out as mod-makers and fans of *Quake 3*.

In Splash Damage's latest game *Enemy Territory: Quake Wars*, players can play as a human, or as an alien Strogg.

A Blood elf character
from *World of Warcraft*.

Many online gamers take part in MMORPGs. This stands for Massively Multiplayer Online Role-Playing Games.

It's a bit of a mouthful, but it means games in which many players play together in a non-stop world.

These worlds often have fantasy themes.

Players can "level up" their characters' skills and collect new weapons and armour.

One of the most famous MMORPGs is *World of Warcraft*. It has over 10 million players.

This online game came from a famous strategy game called *Warcraft: Orcs and Humans*.

An Orc

In the online game of *World of Warcraft*, players create characters on either the side of the Alliance or the Horde.

Players then choose their race, such as human, undead, Draenei or Blood elves. They also choose their class, such as a shape-changing druid, or an axe-wielding warrior.

After that, there's the huge world of Azeroth to explore and quest through.

The Draenei are an alien race who have been at war with the race of Orcs for many years.

CHAPTER 4

GAMING AS A SPORT

Online gaming has gone from being just a hobby. Now it is an actual competitive sport known as eSports.

ESports have tournaments all over the world. Players can win money and other prizes.

Fatal1ty in action

One of the most famous eSportsmen is American Johnathan "Fatal1ty" Wendel.

Fatal1ty has won more major gaming tournaments than any other gamer on the planet.

Like any professional athlete, Fatal1ty trains every day – for up to 10 hours!

He also watches videos of himself in action to help him improve.

Fatal1ty plays against students taking part in a video gaming course.

Fatal1ty is a spokesperson for eSports. He also has his own range of gaming equipment.

CHAPTER 5

GAMES AND THE MOVIES

Many games have been made into movies, such as *Tomb Raider* and *Hitman*.

Not many have been very successful. However, movie-makers still want to link up with videogames because they are such big business.

The biggest entertainment product ever is a videogame for over 18s – *Grand Theft Auto IV*. It earned over £168 million in just 24 hours.

That's more than the movie *Spider-Man 3* and the book *Harry Potter and the Deathly Hallows*, earned in their first 24 hours, put together!

Lara Croft, the star of *Tomb Raider*, is one of the most famous videogame characters in the world.

Movie-makers are also lending their skills to games.

The actor Andy Serkis was the dramatic director for the PS3 exclusive *Heavenly Sword*.

He also voiced the main villain, King Bohan.

Andy Serkis played Gollum in *Lord of the Rings*.

King Bohan

CHAPTER 6

VIOLENCE IN GAMES

Violence in games is a hot topic that many people have opinions about.

In 1997, *Carmageddon* was the first game to be banned in the UK.

In *Carmageddon* players could run over human characters with cars.

The game was later released in the UK with an 18 age-rating. In some parts of the world the human characters had to be replaced by robots or zombies.

Violence in games – have your say...

- Is it OK to include violence in games as long as they have an age-rating?

- When people look at an age-rating, do you think they know what they might see or play in a game?

Age-ratings tell us who a game is right for.

The age-ratings are decided based on the game's content. For example, does the game show violence? Do characters use bad language?

CHAPTER 7 : MAKING GAMES

Once, games used to be made by just a couple of people. Now a team might include designers, artists, programmers, writers and sound engineers.

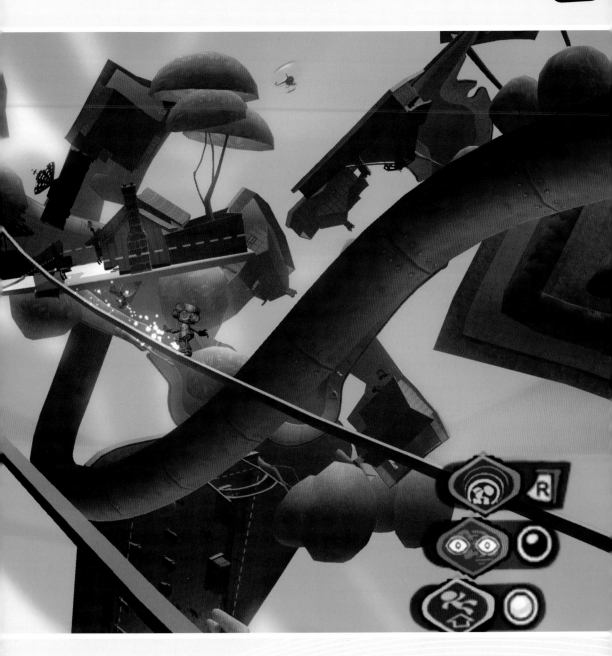

Most games take between two and three years to develop.

One of the most important parts of designing a game is coming up with USPs (Unique Selling Points).

USPs are all the great things that make the game stand out from the crowd.

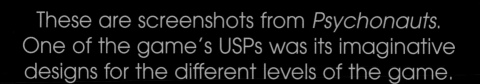

These are screenshots from *Psychonauts*. One of the game's USPs was its imaginative designs for the different levels of the game.

Psychonauts is an action-adventure game. It is about a young boy called Raz and his adventures at a summer camp for kids with psychic powers.

Most developers show their game's design to publishers during a "pitch".

If a publisher likes the idea, they will pay the developers to produce the game.

However, amazing games can come from unusual places.

Princess No Knees in *Narbacular Drop*

Narbacular Drop was a free game. It was created by students at DigiPen. At this American college, students can learn games design.

It featured a Princess called "No Knees" because she couldn't jump.

When the games company Valve saw the game, they liked it a lot!

They liked it so much, they offered the students the ultimate dream gaming job – a place on Valve's team!

A screenshot from *Portal*

Valve remade the game as *Portal* – one of the best action-puzzle games ever!

During a game's development the design team will continue to design the gameplay.

They will design things such as missions, boss fights and even combat.

Artists will create the game's visuals. They create everything from characters, to textures, such as bricks.

Programmers create the game's "engine". This makes all the parts of a game run together.

Sound engineers and composers create the sound effects and music.

Writers write the game's story and the characters' speech.

Testers play-test the game. Could this be the best job in the world? Try playing the same level of a game for eight hours when it's full of bugs!

When the game is finished, developers say it has "gone gold".

An artist at work

It is getting easier for small development teams to release games.

Xbox Live Market Place and Valve's Steam mean games can be released without having a big team and lots of money.

Valve's Steam allows you to buy and download games straight onto your PC.

Working on *Uplink*

Packing games

Introversion Software started as three university friends. The three friends created a game called *Uplink*. They did all the work – even packing up the games to send to customers!

Their second game, *Darwinia*, was picked up by Steam. They helped Introversion get money to create new games.

Introversion is now a team of 11 people. They say Steam helped to make their company a success.

Darwinia's look and level design recreates the look of old arcade games such as *Space Invaders*.

NEED TO KNOW WORDS

age-rating A rating and symbol given to a videogame to tell buyers what age of player it is suitable for.

clan A team of players who game together.

console An electronic unit for playing games on.

dramatic director A person in charge of directing the voice actors in a game.

druid An ancient priest. In fairytales, druids sometimes have magical powers.

editor A piece of software which allows you to design a game or parts of a game.

forum The place on a gaming website where players can chat to each other.

FPS (First-Person Shooter) A game which is played through the eyes of a character.

MMORPG (Massively Multiplayer Online Role- Playing Game) A role-playing game played online with lots of players.

modem A device for sending electronic data.

multiplayer The part of a game that can be played by lots of players at once.

objective A goal.

opponent Someone who you play a game against.

peripheral A device, such as a steering wheel, that can be plugged into a console and used to control a game.

professional Someone who does something for money.

programmer A person who writes computer programmes.

prototype The first model or design of something.

psychic A person with special powers, such as the ability to read minds or see into the future.

tournament A big competition.

GET INTO MAKING GAMES

If you are interested in making games, the Skillset games website has some great advice: *http://www.skillset.org/games/*

There are many roles in games development, all with their own skills. But you don't have to be a big team to create great games. Get involved with online gaming communities and take part in mod and map-making.

Who knows? You might create the next *Narbacular Drop*.

Good luck!

VIDEOGAMES ONLINE

Websites
http://www.introversion.co.uk/
Read about Introversion Software here

http://www.bbc.co.uk/blast/games/
Games to play and information about videogames

http://www.fatal1ty.com/
The website of professional eSportsman Fatal1ty

INDEX